My Journey:

Experiencing the Abuse,
Navigating the Aftermath,
Finding Hope and Healing

My Journey:

Experiencing the Abuse, Navigating the Aftermath, Finding Hope and Healing

by SCW

A story of hope by a survivor of
childhood sexual abuse
written for fellow survivors
and those who love them

For you ...

I wrote this book about my own journey for you if you experienced the horrors of childhood sexual abuse or know someone who did. I am so sorry that any of us have to continue to deal with the lingering effects years after the abuse ends. I know the terrible realities you are facing for I, too, endured physical, emotional, and sexual abuse at the hands of my grandfather for thirteen or fourteen years and have been dealing with the aftermath for more than thirty-five years. I survived, and you or your loved one will, too. I am grateful to my husband ("Garth"), my DC pastor/counselor ("Carol"), my Louisiana therapist ("Maggie"), my sisters ("Cheryl" and "Mary"), and special friends (BF, RF, NC, LB, LGS, LL, MG) who have walked with me, encouraged me, cared for me, and held me to help me feel safe – literally and figuratively.

My journey isn't over, but the path has become much easier to navigate. The good news is that what Carol keeps telling me really is true: the good days become more frequent, and the bad days become less bad. Hang in there. In these pages, I tell my story. I've always been a writer, and, as I've walked the scary path of figuring out what all this stuff means for me, I've spent many hours typing on my computer. There are stories that I've written to help me figure things out and letters that I've written as I explore new realities. They are presented roughly chronologically. My hope is that you can find comfort in knowing that you are not alone. Sadly, far too many of us have experienced such abuse. May God bless you on your own healing journey.

SCW

Northern Virginia, USA

March 2007

Table of Contents

Chapter 1: An Awful Truth
September, 1997 – March, 1998

Mine is a journey of coming to accept the truth about what happened to me and who and what I am. If you have not gone through it yourself, you may find it extremely difficult to understand how someone could live through years and years of abuse and not have clear recollections of what happened.[1] In fact, if it hadn't happened to me, I'm not sure I could believe it myself. I know there are those who do not accept that a "recovered memory" can be valid or true. I am not telling my story to try to convince them that they're wrong. I do know the world is not simply black and white; there's a whole lot of gray. It is possible that some "recovered memories" are not true; I have come to accept for myself that at least some are *very true*. This is my story.

It began with the eyes. As I closed my eyes to go to sleep at night, all I could see was these scary eyes. I didn't know whose eyes they were, but I knew they were terrifying. I had started working with Maggie[2] two months earlier. A friend had recommended Maggie to me after I shared with him the fact that my older neighbor had made me have sex with him multiple times beginning when I was about ten years old. I thought I was seeing Maggie to work through my feelings of guilt over having let Kendrick do those things to me so I could have a more fulfilling sexual relationship with my husband. Then the scary eyes started appearing every

---

[1] I will leave it to others to debate whether or not "recovered memories" are valid. Jim Hopper has a website that presents scientific evidence to support repression as a coping mechanism (http://www.jimhopper.com/memory/), and Jennifer Freyd lays out reasons why repression may occur in her book *Betrayal Trauma: The Logic of Forgetting Childhood Sexual Abuse* (Harvard University Press, 1996). What I *know* is that I desperately wish that none of this had happened to me and my sisters believe me. If you are questioning your own memory, examine your motives. In general, we don't invent things that make us feel bad.

[2] All of the names have been changed. Sadly, though, the story is true.

time I closed my own eyes. I couldn't figure out what they meant or see the face behind them.

It was September of 1997. My daughter was in first grade, and my son was almost two years old. I had just earned tenure and a promotion at the university where I taught. I was exhausted because I wasn't getting a lot of sleep. I wracked my brain trying to figure out what those eyes meant and/or why they were so terrifying and/or to whom they belonged. Slowly it began to come to me. I saw flashes of the face. The face looked like my grandfather's. Every time I tried to go to sleep, I saw the same dark, harsh, scary eyes and felt sheer terror as they came closer and closer to me. I couldn't understand why the face looked like my grandfather's face – surely his eyes weren't that mean and scary, and surely seeing them wouldn't evoke such strong feelings of fear in me. Then I began to see flashes or glimpses of other things, and they were even scarier than the eyes.

I did not want to believe what I was seeing; it was too awful to comprehend. Yet, I had to acknowledge that the eyes were so terrifying because they meant that he was coming down the hall to do awful things to me and to make me do things I did not want to do. At night, as he came down the hall toward my room, the nightlight in the hall – it had been placed there to help me feel safe – would reflect in his eyes. When I saw those eyes, I knew he was coming, and that was a very scary thing. That nightlight did not help me feel safe; instead it illuminated the dark and horrible things to come.

I knew that, when he got to my room, he was going to make me do things I did not want to do. Sometimes he made me suck on his thing. (It started when I was so young that I didn't even know that it was called a penis.) I didn't like that because, after I sucked on it for a while, stuff would come out the end. I thought it was pee, and I was afraid that it was going to make me sick. Other times, he would stick his thing inside me and/or rubbed it around on me until the stuff came out the end. When it came out, he would tell me that I had to clean it up or I'd be in big trouble; then he would remind me that I couldn't use any towels or toilet paper because my grandmother might notice and wonder why I had needed them. So, I would have to figure out a way to clean up the mess without letting anyone know.

As I struggled to grasp the concept that my grandfather might have done these things to me, I prayed that it was not true. I wondered how in the world I could have buried such knowledge for twenty years; I desperately hoped that I could attribute all those horrible things to Kendrick. At the same time, I *knew* they were true: my grandfather had sexually abused me – over and over and over and over and over. That was *incest*, and I hated the idea that I had been a party to incestuous acts. But, no matter how many different approaches I used to try to prove to myself that it could not possibly be true, I ultimately had to begin to accept a worse truth than that of a neighbor making me do things that I did not want to do.

Maggie knew I hadn't been sleeping, but I hadn't told her the real truth about why. I didn't want to have to admit that my grandfather had done such awful things to me. But, denial wasn't working; I wasn't sleeping. I knew I had to tell Maggie what I was seeing and what I feared it meant. I hoped that she'd tell me that it couldn't possibly be true. I felt awful going to my appointment that day. I dreaded telling her. I didn't want to have to admit that a thing as awful as incest had happened in my family – to me; I didn't want her to think I was a bad person; and, I didn't want it to be true. I wanted her to tell me that it couldn't be true.

As she watched me struggle to tell her that I suspected that my grandfather had sexually abused me, her eyes reflected compassion and grace – so very different from the scary eyes that came down the hall at night. Her initial reaction was not disgust; the scary thing was that her initial response was to tell me that it could be true. Since there was no magic she could use to discern the truth, she assured me that she would walk with me as I grappled with the idea that it might be true.

He was dead, so I couldn't ask him if it was true. Had he still been alive, he might have denied it even if it was true. He kept it hidden, and he convinced me that it was in my best interest not to tell anyone, either. So, it was going to be difficult to find incontrovertible evidence to prove or disprove what I feared to be true. In March of 1998, I decided to risk telling one of my sisters, Cheryl. That was a scary thing to do. She could have told me that there was no way such a thing was true and been so offended that I could even suggest that our grandfather had done these horrible things that she would see to it that I was no longer welcome at any family functions. It was a terrifying proposition, but I hoped she could help me find the truth.

We lived about four hours apart by car. My plan was to drive over to see her so I could tell her face-to-face. I wanted to make sure that she would be home (so I wouldn't have driven eight hours round-trip for nothing), but I was too afraid to call her to ask her if she was going to be home. My dear, sweet, supportive husband called her. When he told her that I wanted to come tell her something, she volunteered to meet me halfway. That is how I came to be sitting in a booth in a Mexican restaurant in an East Texas town trying to find the courage to go ahead and say what I needed to say.

Some part of me desperately hoped that she would tell me I was wrong and point out something I was missing to convince me I was wrong. I told her that she didn't have to believe me, but that I had to tell her something.[3] When I finally got it out, her immediate response was to tell me she was very sad to hear it – sad for me that I had to live through such awful experiences. After considering it a little longer, she added that,

---

[3] Telling is scary. Maggie had helped me plan what I wanted to say. If you're about to tell someone for the first time, please be prepared for any response. It helped me to I first tell the listener that they were free to think anything they wanted to think. Then I asked them that their first oral response *not* be that they didn't believe me. It was okay for them not to believe me; I just didn't want that to be the first thing I heard them say to me. I have not run into anyone who did not believe me yet.

in retrospect, my revelation made so many things make sense. Then she noted that she was sad that she hadn't figured it out back then.

I froze. Here was confirmation of my worst fears: she believed it to be true, too.

She suggested that I should tell our other sister, Mary, too, and she volunteered to meet me at Mary's house (who lived four hours away from Cheryl and five hours away from me) whenever I wanted to tell her. While that was further affirmation that Cheryl believed me, it was also another very scary proposition. What if Mary didn't concur with Cheryl's assessment of the situation? Then where would I be?

The following weekend, Cheryl met me at Mary's house. My parents' fiftieth wedding anniversary was coming up, so we told Mary that we were coming to work on plans for the big reception. It made sense to meet at Mary's house because she lived in the same town as my parents. At an appropriate time, Cheryl told Mary that I needed to tell her something. Cheryl added that it was hard to hear, but that she had heard it and believed it to be true.

I told Mary what I had told Cheryl the weekend before. Mary's immediate response was also to believe me without any hesitation; she reaffirmed that knowing that he had done those things to me made several other things make a whole lot more sense.

So, when I speak of the "truth" in my story, I admit that I don't have tangible evidence to support my belief that it is the truth. All I can say is that I desperately wish it was not true, and, at the same time, I _know_ that it *is* the truth.

It's an awful truth.

Chapter 2: The Harsh Realities
1962 – January 26, 1976

Monday, January 26, 1976, was the day he died. He was my grandfather – my mother's father. Our families are supposed to love us, to care for us, to protect us – especially when we are vulnerable little children. He didn't do that; he abused me sexually, emotionally, and physically beginning when I was just two years old. It stopped only when he died: Monday, January 26, 1976.

Well, the abuse itself stopped when he died. The aftermath reverberates still today – more than thirty-one years later. The good news for me is that I have learned that it was not my fault and that I am a good person. Here are the harsh realities.

I had some really bad stuff happen to me when I was a kid. It didn't happen just once, nor was it limited to just a few months or even just a year or two: he did these awful, awful things to me over and over and over and over and over and over and over and over and over and over and over and over again and again and again for thirteen years or so. He controlled me by telling me what a terrible, awful, bad person I was. He started when I was very young and impressionable, and he kept telling me the same things: (1) I was a terrible, awful, bad person; (2) If anybody ever found out how truly terrible, awful, and bad I was then I would be in *huge* trouble; (3) He was smart enough to hide my badness and he would as long as I did what he asked; (4) If I ever did tell, nobody would believe me and they would know what a bad person I was because only terrible, awful, bad little girls did the things he made me do.

He told me about my innate badness so many times – beginning when I was so young – that I simply accepted it as an absolute truth. When he died, I was not relieved that he couldn't hurt me anymore; instead, I was absolutely terrified that people would soon discover what a terrible, awful, bad person I was.

Thanks to his lies, I spent the next thirty years of my life doing my best to figure out what a "good" person would do and then doing it. I knew a day would come when my badness would be uncovered for all to see. In the meantime, I tried to do the best I could. Here's my current understanding of the chronology of the things that he did to me.[4]

Year 1, 1962: I think it started in the summer when I was two years old – about thirty-one months – just a little girl. My grandparents lived about 30 miles away. Cheryl and Mary tell me that we visited their lake house fairly often. I have very little recollection of this place, but I know that it was isolated. It began here with him taking me to "secret" places and showing me his penis. He made me touch it or lick it – even put the end of it in my mouth. *I was two years old!* I think he even jerked off and made me watch. That's when his eyes would get really scary; his eyes would get really mean and scary when penis was big and hard and stuff came out the end.

Little did I know that those eyes – and the man behind them would terrorize me for years to come.

***

Year 2, 1963: They were still living at their lake house. I think it was about this time that he began to stick things inside where my tee-tee came out (my vagina, but I certainly didn't know what it was called then). It wasn't always his penis - sometimes it was a ruler or a coke bottle or maybe a stick that he found. He told me that he was doing this to help me understand that there was plenty of room in there for his penis so I didn't need to be scared about him sticking his penis in me. He reiterated that the only thing that I had to fear was having someone find out what I was doing. Even though he told me I didn't need to be, I was still scared when he stuck things inside me. They hurt.

---

[4] The mind is a strange thing. Memories are not necessarily stored chronologically, and some memories can be buried for a long time. They can be hazy and confusing when they're revisited.

I turned 4 in October of 1963. I was having recurrent kidney and/or bladder infections – probably from all of the things he was sticking inside me.

He was doing all these things to me, and I was just a sweet little girl with long curly hair.

***

Year 3, 1964: Even though they were still living out of town, they came to see us more and more often. My mother was their only child, so they didn't have any other grandchildren to visit. The trip was only 30 miles, and gas was really cheap then: ~8¢ a gallon.

I continued to have persistent kidney and/or bladder infections.[5] I had my tonsils removed in 1964. I think the doctors thought my tonsils were the source of my recurrent infections. In truth, I hid the pain when I tee-teed because I didn't want to get in trouble; even after they took my tonsils out, I still had kidney and/or bladder infections.

The doctors were stumped; they didn't understand why taking my tonsils out hadn't stopped the infections. I got in trouble for not wiping myself the right way when I went to the bathroom. I couldn't tell them the truth; then everybody would find out what a terrible, awful, bad person I was and I would be in *huge* trouble.

He kept sticking things in me: his penis a lot – and then he would tee-tee in me. (He actually was ejaculating, but I thought it was pee.) It was messy, and it hurt. And, it happened lots of times.

***

Year 4, 1965: They moved to the same town where I lived. Cheryl was a freshman in high school. My parents were busy with their work; they had a lot of weekday evening commitments. Cheryl had her driver's license,

---

[5] My sisters believe that the recurrent bladder infections (and subsequent loss of one of my kidneys) are further evidence that he really did do these things to me.

and she and Mary would go out and do their own things. (They are less than two years apart in age; I am 6 and 8 years younger than my sisters.) My grandparents would come stay with me a lot. He kept sticking things – and himself – inside me.

I turned 6 in October, and one of my kidneys was removed in November. The doctors found that it had become necrotic from repeated infections. He got so mad at me when I had to have the surgery. The truth is that the hospital was my sanctuary. He didn't hurt me as long as I was there. I was sad when they told me I was well enough to go home.

***

Year 5, 1966: Early in the year, he couldn't stick his penis in my bottom because I had had the operation, so he stuck it in my mouth a lot and really hard – much harder than earlier times. He took me inside his travel trailer that was parked in his back yard and jammed his penis in my mouth; he did it so hard that I felt like I was suffocating. His body overwhelmed me, and his penis and the stuff that came out of it gagged me. I couldn't breathe. I was afraid I was going to die. The first time he did this, I bit his penis to make him move so I could breathe. He got really, really mad at me and hit me on the side of my head hard enough that I saw stars.

After that very scary first time, he did the same thing a lot more, but I never bit him again. He kept telling me not to tell anybody; I was totally convinced that I'd be in big, big trouble if anybody ever found out.

***

Years 6 – 12, 1967 – 1973: This was seven years in hell. Among the scary things he did to me during these years was a terrifying Halloween outing – it scared me for reasons completely unrelated to traditional Halloween pranks. He took me trick-or-treating. When we reached a poorly lit yard, he pulled me into the yard, stood behind a bush, dropped his pants, and made me put his penis in my mouth. I was so afraid that someone would catch us and I would be in big, big trouble.

Cheryl graduated from high school in 1969; Mary did, too, in 1971. I was left alone with my grandparents so many times. My parents had evening commitments or traveled over the weekend quite often. He *always* did terrible things to me when I stayed with them. Many times, it would be at night.

The bedroom that I stayed in at my grandparents' house was at the opposite end of a long hall from theirs – the hall with the nightlight. The furniture in my room included a dresser with a large mirror that faced the hall and reflected those scary, scary eyes. I could see them coming all the way down the hall. I wanted to turn the nightlight off. I thought maybe he wouldn't come down the hall if it was too dark for him to see. My grandmother insisted that the nightlights stay on; she told me that my grandfather needed them to find his way to the bathroom in the middle of the night. (I couldn't tell her where he was really going when he left their room.)

He never let me close the door to my bedroom. I wanted to because I thought it might keep him out. When I went to bed each night at their house, I would lie in bed waiting – terrified of what I knew was coming. Too often I saw the reflection of the nightlight in his scary eyes in the mirror on the dresser. I tried to find places to hide, but the closet was full of boxes and there were more under the bed. There was nowhere to hide. The mean, scary eyes in the hall meant he was going to do mean, scary things to me.

It was also during these years that Kendrick, my older neighbor started making me do things, too. The lies my grandfather had told me again and again and again and again convinced me that I was a terrible, awful, bad person. I was afraid that Kendrick had somehow figured out how bad I was, too. Since doing scary things with my grandfather helped "protect" me, I hoped Kendrick would also "protect" me if I did similar things with him. A few years after it started, Kendrick moved and he didn't do anything else to me.

Meanwhile, my grandfather kept doing things to me. There were times when he took me into his garage. When we were in the garage, my grandmother was often just inside the door making us lunch. I was so afraid she was going to hear us and find out. He also took me to the shed out in his backyard; I was afraid the neighbors would learn the truth about what was happening. One time when he had taken me out to the shed, his dog started barking a lot. My grandfather got very mad at the dog and kicked him really hard to make him shut up. The dog never barked at us again.

The trailer was also parked in has backyard. It was an Airstream trailer; it was so hot in the summer and so cold in the winter. The temperature didn't seem to matter to my grandfather; he had his way with me in the steamy heat and the bone-chilling cold.

I started high school in the fall of 1973; it still didn't end. It only got worse.

***

Years 13 – 14, 1974 – 1975: I don't know why I divided the years like this (1967 – 1973 and 1974 – 1975). After all, I could have just said 1967 – 1975. I don't know.

I think that it was sometime in 1974 that I started wondering if he should be doing these things to me or not. Maybe that's why. Or, maybe it's that Kendrick moved away in the summer of 1973, so these years feel like something different to me as I look back. Maybe it was during these years that I had my first period. I have no idea when I had my first period; my sisters believe that's more damning evidence.

Maybe it's that 1973 – 1974 marked my freshman year in high school, so that's why split it this way. I rode a Greyhound bus for six hours to visit Cheryl while her husband was away on business in the summer of 1973; they had gotten married in August of 1972. That week with my sister was a wonderful respite. I got my driver's license in October of 1975 when I turned 16.

Late in 1975, a family from church asked me to babysit their children while they attended a party. My parents were out of town, so I was staying at my grandparents' house. I had my driver's license; I drove myself over to the babysitting job. My grandfather was mad about that. He wanted to drive me over there. It was pretty far away, so I was scared that he was going to do something to me on the way if he drove. Fortunately, my grandmother wanted him to stay home with her, so he didn't take me over there. The parents for whom I was babysitting stayed out quite late; I didn't get back to my grandparents' house until after 1 a.m.

My grandfather was furious. He met me at the front door and told me that I was going to be in big trouble if I didn't do what he wanted me to do right then. Instead of complying, I found the courage to ask him if he really thought it was okay to be doing those things to me. That made him even angrier. He tried to force me into the bedroom. I told him I didn't want to do those things any more. His eyes blazed with anger.

I couldn't win. He had his way with me.

***

1976, the end: Less than a month after the late-night confrontation, he died. I'll never forget the day or the date: Monday, January 26, 1976.

He could no longer hurt me physically, but I was wounded in other ways, too. I was scared people were going to figure out how bad I was since he wasn't there to help hide my badness anymore.

***

March, 2007: I have only recently come to understand that these things happened to me – not because I deserved them, not because I wasn't smart enough to figure out a way to make him stop, not because I did something wrong or didn't do something right, not because of anything that I did or didn't do. These things happened to me because of him – not because of me.

I'm still working on believing both parts: (1) all of these awful, awful things happened to me (2) not because I deserved them or couldn't get away – but because he did them to me.

I am where I am today because I got through it somehow. Yes, these terrible, terrible things happened to me – and they were awful. No one ever deserves to be subjected to such horrendous deeds. However, they didn't happen to me because I did anything at all to deserve them; they happened to me simply because I was there.

Chapter 3: My Work with Maggie
July, 1997 – May, 2000

I graduated from high school in the top ten percent of my class. I went to college and earned a BA in English. I worked at a small family-owned business[6] for a couple of years and went back to school and earned an MBA. I worked for a small consulting firm for several years and was promoted to Director of my own division. By many external measures, I was "successful." However, I knew I was hiding an awful truth about my badness; I did my best to appear to be "good."

I met a guy, Garth. He was smart and had beautiful eyes – his eyes were never scary. I had dated other guys before; he was the first one who didn't try to talk me into having sex with him. I was still working at the consulting firm, and he moved to another state. I sadly concluded that we would never be more than friends.

Then, one night, he called me really late; I had already gone to bed. This was in the days before caller id, so I didn't know who was calling. I assumed it was a wrong number. Instead, when I answered, it was the cute guy with the pretty eyes. He was calling to tell me that he was moving. We had been living in towns about 1,000 miles apart; now he was moving to a town about two hundred miles away from mine. Having grown up in Texas, I considered two hundred miles to be close enough to drive over for a weekend – or just for a day. I couldn't get back to sleep; I hoped that his moving nearer would give us another chance.

It did. We were married in June of 1988. I moved to the small town where he lived, and Garth and I both taught at the university there. He already had his doctorate; in fact, we met while he was in graduate school. The university administration encouraged me to pursue one, too.

---

[6] *My* family did not own the business. In fact, I was the only person who worked there who was *not* a member of the owner's family.

Our daughter was born in 1990, and I earned my PhD in 1994. We had moved for my schooling, but we returned to our jobs in the fall of 1994. We both earned tenure. Our son was born in 1995. I was elected to leadership positions in the faculty governance structure; I was nominated to serve on a statewide faculty council. Again, by all external appearances, I was successful. I had a wonderful husband, two beautiful kids, and a good job. We lived in my dream house.

In truth, I was miserable. I had always remembered the things Kendrick did to me, and I wondered if I needed to find a therapist to help me work through some of the hurt and pain. A friend had also been sexually abused as a child, and he told me that the things Kendrick had done to me were abusive. That was a revelation to me. He encouraged me to go see Maggie and gave me her phone number. I carried it around for several weeks before finding the courage to give her a call.

My first appointment with Maggie was on July 8, 1997. I thought I was there to talk about the many awful things Kendrick had done to me. My stated goal was to learn to like sex so I could enjoy it with my husband.

I didn't tell her how bad I was because I accepted that as a fact that I would have to live with for the rest of my life. I believed that I needed to hide my badness from her so she would be willing to work with me. I was afraid she would figure out how bad I was and invite me to leave her practice.

I told her about Kendrick, and she told me that was sexual abuse. Even thought my friend had tried to tell me the same thing, it was a revelation to me to hear that from Maggie. I had always assumed that it was somehow my fault that Kendrick had done those things. Maggie told me that he was older and there was a power imbalance – and that it was sexual abuse. She specialized in working with survivors of childhood sexual abuse. In fact, she ran a group for survivors one night a week, and she invited me to join the group in August of 1997. As part of the group process, each member was invited to tell her story. At the time, the only story I knew was Kendrick; that's the story I told.

In retrospect, it is easy to see that I had stuffed all of the memories of the sexual abuse – whether from my grandfather or from Kendrick – into a box labeled "Kendrick." I simply was not ready to deal with the fact that my own grandfather had done far worse things to me over many more years than Kendrick had. I think that looking at the "Kendrick" box with Maggie stirred up the awful truth. As August became September, I grew more and more tense. Then I started seeing those eyes and feeling the awful terror every time I closed my own eyes.

Slowly, the image became clearer: it was my grandfather who had done so many of these awful things to me. I fought against that version of the truth, but, in the end, the real truth became clearer. By March of 1998, I was ready to tell Cheryl and Mary.

My time with Maggie was hard. I would get so scared and so sad, and I would lash out at Maggie. I "fired" her several times only to ask her to take me back within hours of firing her. I lashed out at perceived injustices. I had been a part of three groups[7]. Near the last session of the third group, I commented that I had "always" done a particular assignment the same way in every group.

She looked at me – in front of the whole group – and asked, "Always?" That was the final straw as far as I was concerned. It felt like she doubted me. I waited a few days and then lashed out with a fury – I said some awful things, and I fired her.

Fifteen minutes later, I was desperate to continue my work with her. I wanted to make amends, so I wrote her a story. This is that story:

"Hi, how are you doing today? Shall we go up?"

It always starts the same way. I think she tries to encourage you, subtly, of course, as she invites you into her room. Up the stairs and

---

[7] Each group met for eight weeks.

to the left – to the room, her office. It is a bright room; it has windows on three walls – but not bright glaring windows, soft windows with blinds and curtains. It is large. After all, she is the Executive Director. She probably has all sorts of external pressures – funding, staffing, maintaining staff morale, working with insurance companies, helping financially-distressed clients get the services they need and deserve. But, for that hour, she is yours – and you are her only concern. There is the desk on one end of the office with the glass top that is too large. I guess it holds more "stuff" that way; however, it is never cluttered, so room on the desktop doesn't really seem to be an issue. The other end of the office is home to the requisite couch (a floral print) and two comfortable swivel rockers (solid green to meld nicely with the floral print). There are tissue boxes discreetly placed within easy reach. Clocks are everywhere – small enough to be unobtrusive and easily dismissed if they need be.

We'll go in and sit down. Maybe I'll try a different seat today. I wonder what she'd read into that. Maybe nothing. After all, *she* is the one who has told me to interpret other's actions positively if I am going to interpret them at all. Maybe she'd think that the changing of the chairs symbolizes a changing of the guard, so to speak – a positive step toward reclaiming some of that lost child that resides within me. You see, I am a survivor of the most insidious of crimes. I was sexually abused as a child. That alone is a most horrible crime, for it happens when one in control, one with power, uses his or her authority to take something sacred and intimate – something that God created so that two can become one – and uses it solely for him or herself. Someone in power took something sacred from me.

For years and years, I tried to claim that the theft had meant nothing. I told myself that it did not really matter. Hey, I had succeeded in life by whatever "typical" measure one wants to use. I graduated in the top 10% of my high school class – not salutatorian like one of my sisters, but still wearing the badge of the National Honor Society – something the other sister could not claim. Of course, they were drum major, cheerleader, homecoming queen, class officers, fraternity sweethearts, University Beauties – and married within days of college graduation to swell guys. After high school, I, too, went to college. I did not join my sisters' sorority – I chose a different path. I was not chosen as a beauty. I was not a fraternity sweetheart. I hardly dated. I finished in four years with an unmarketable liberal arts degree. I did not get married right away. I did get a job.

The college degree and job weren't enough. I entered graduate school. I moved back home. What a blow to my parents who had begun enjoying the freedoms of doing what they wished when they wished. I successfully completed my masters' degree – with a perfect 4.0, no less. I took a job in another town. I met a guy – a really neat guy – in the church choir. We were good friends, and he did not use me. Then he moved away.

I became a Division Director in the firm where I worked. Is that enough to be a "success"? No. I still was not married. And the childhood abuse meant nothing. How could it? I was pretty normal. Doesn't everyone have self-doubts? Doesn't everyone think that everybody else is better than him or herself? Doesn't everyone fear the day that their "true" nature is revealed? I knew that, if anyone at the firm discovered the truth about me, they would fire me in a heartbeat.

Then the really nice guy called one night. He had taken a job in a town not too far away. Be still, my heart. What are you trying to tell me, God? We were married within a year. I got a job as an instructor at the local college. My students thought I was really good at what I did. Married. Teaching at the college. Surely now I was a success.

No, that was not enough. So, we had a child, and I earned a doctorate. Well, of course, anybody could have done either one. I'm pretty certain that there are many better mothers than I, and the Ph.D. is much more about persistence and perseverance than about ability. I became a "tenure-track" faculty member. We had another child. I earned tenure, was elected Faculty Senate President by my peers, and was chosen as Assistant Dean. Success? Hardly. I mean, how can it be a success to have everyone completely fooled. If I'm ever found out, I'm sunk.

One summer day, I called her for the first time. She specializes in survivors of childhood sexual abuse. She came highly recommended. Of course, I was doing it for him. For that really neat guy who never abused me. He protected me – even when I tempted him to violate me. You see, *I* wasn't worth all the money, the time, the energy, the effort. *He* was.

So, she came to the waiting area, introduced herself, and invited me up to the room. The room with 1,000 demons – and one God. The room in which I revealed my deepest, darkest secrets to her. The room where the groups met. The small group. Then the really large group. Then the middle-sized group.

Each week, I'd drive to her office, go in, sit down in the reception area, and wait. She'd pop her head through the door and say, "Hi, how are you doing today? Shall we go up?"

Some days the steps were really steep; other times I could climb without noticing. Then, as summer turned to fall, the inner walls – walls I had built as a child to hide the truth even from myself – began to crumble and fall. I could hardly get out of the car. The stairs were really, really steep that day. I had to say it out loud. I had to see what she would say. Surely she would be so disgusted that she would refer me to someone else.

It began as a cry from deep within: "I can't do it. I just can't do it." I did not know what it was that I could not do. I only knew that I could not do it. As the truth emerged from its self-imposed sanctum, it became eyes that would not leave my view as I closed my own eyes and tried to go to sleep. I didn't understand the eyes. I did not recognize the face behind the eyes. I did not recognize the face because I did not want to know the truth. Then I *knew* the face.

You see, it wasn't just someone in a position of power who had sexually molested me. It goes beyond insidious. The depths of the wound are so great that the child in me cannot comprehend them, for she can't believe that he would do such a thing. The adult within me could not believe that the unthinkable could be true. No matter how hard the little girl tries to protect me from myself and no matter how hard the adult tries to deny it, the truth is there. My grandfather sexually abused me – probably for a very long time in my life. He was supposed to love me – to protect me from the horrors of the world. He didn't. He stole that most sacred of divine gifts from me – in that front bedroom. What a sorry little bastard.

Now it is hands and a child caressed against a man's chest that will not leave me as I seek sleep. I do not know what the hands mean, nor do I understand the caress, nor do I know the age of the child. There are also flashes of green. I do not know what they mean.

In the meantime, I try to go on with my life. There are work pressures, parent pressures, spouse pressures, family-of-origin pressures, and internal pressures. Herbs help control the pressures. Cigarettes help, too, but they are too nasty to be of any long-term use. Of course, there's the nicotine gum. It's almost as good as the cigarettes. What have I become? A herb-addicted, nicotine-addicted body that moves through life trying to say the right things at the right time. That gets hard. The work pressures escalate. Then comes the explosion.

Of course, I can't explode at work. They'd figure me out, and I'd get fired. I can't explode at home. He deserves better than a sexually-abused, herb-addicted, nicotine-addicted, asexual exploding wife. Plus, the children deserve better than an explosion. I can't explode in the direction of my parents – hell, I'd prefer never to have to deal with them again – why go to the trouble of exploding in their direction. I can't explode internally – the consequences could be too disastrous for those I love. So, I explode at her.

"Hi, how are you doing today? Shall we go up?"

Hell, no. *We* aren't going to do a fucking thing. *She* is going to see how angry I can be. You see, she should have never said "Always?" so innocently that night in front of all those other people. *She* was supposed to *know* that this was my third group – *she* had facilitated every one of them. And, that's not the issue at all, is it. No, and the explosion comes anyway. With full fury – and intent to hurt. After all, she knows my most intimate secrets, and she questioned my veracity in front of those others.

The mind reading begins. Interpreting another's intent with no information beyond the visible actions. She told me to interpret positively. I don't. I believe that she has become bored with me, with my piddling little case history. After all, there were only five or six perpetrators at various points in my life. On the surface, I appear to have come through it all very well. A terrific husband. Two wonderful children. A doctorate. A good job. Good friends. What problems can I have left? It is time to get on with life – and to quit taking up her time. So, I can only believe that the intent is to hurt, to drive me away so she can get on with her ministry to those who really need her services. Clearly she has decided that it is time for me to stop coming to see her to whine, to be a crutch, to do whatever it is I do in that room with the floral print couch and green chairs. So, she makes the remark. "Always?" She questions me in front of the others. I wait a few days, and I explode.

Then, I have to retract some of the explosion. I'll go to the last group to show her that I am bigger than that remark. She badgers me about my mood. Fuck all that. I just won't see her again.

Of course, I have to see her again. I need to apologize. She didn't deserve the explosion. Maybe I didn't deserve the abuse. My grandfather never apologized. Kendrick never apologized. The others never apologized. I'm bigger and better than any of them. I will go apologize.

I need more than that. I need her back in my life. I need that crutch. I need that room. I need to know who I am. I need to know that I am okay. I need to *believe* that I am okay. I need her to help me get there.

I'll drive to her office tomorrow. I'm sure I'll feel heavier and heavier as I get closer to the place. I'll get out of my car. I'll go into the reception area and wait.

She is ready and willing to forgive and move forward. I want to move forward, too. I'm not sure I can forgive myself. While I'm waiting, I'll hear her come downstairs. She will probably have been up with another client. She'll see that person out. She'll check to make sure all is okay downstairs. Then she'll poke her head through the door and say, "Hi, how are you doing today? Shall we go up?"

I'll go up. I don't know where I'll sit. I'm ready to make changes, and I want to be safe. I believe she'll help me if I let her. I want to let her.

Let the journey begin.

She graciously welcomed me back into her office – into her presence. She shared my journey with me for almost three years. During my time with Maggie, I got in touch with my inner child. She was trying to protect me by keeping the awful truths hidden; ultimately, though, they were too painful to keep at bay. It was hard for that little girl to be rejected as I learned more about the awful things my grandfather had done to me. I didn't want to know more, *and* I didn't want to abandon that sweet little girl who had done her best to make it through the horrors of her childhood. It's hard when you don't believe in yourself. At the same time, I didn't like the things I was learning about myself. I don't think anyone wants to have been molested repeatedly by her grandfather; I don't think anyone wants to have been told over and over and over again that they're worthless, no one will believe them – or believe *in* them. He also convinced me that it didn't matter if it hurt because nobody cared if I was hurting. I needed to say it out loud. I used this story to help me do that:

"Hi! How are you today? Shall we go up?"

I believe I've told you that it always starts the same – the subtle, gentle, optimistic delivery. It's always the same – no matter how she feels. She even came in from her sick bed one afternoon and managed to greet me the same way. I wasn't as nice. I told her I'd have been pissed if she hadn't come in that afternoon. That really isn't a very nice way to greet or treat something so precious.

Gee – I don't think I'll want to go up this day. I fear that the steps will be really, really steep. The forecast calls for rain, so it could be a struggle against the elements just to make it to the door. Then I'll have to sit and wait. I'll have to think about anything but what I'm there to discuss. Actually, it will be pretty easy to avoid the subject – I've managed to do so quite nicely for over thirty years. And, I wish it had never, ever, ever surfaced. And, maybe I couldn't live if it hadn't.

Anyway, she knows what I will have come to say on this day. I tried to say it the last time we were together, and I couldn't get it out. I guess I was hoping that by not saying it I could make it not be true. Unfortunately, silence really isn't golden. Silence can't wash away the truth. So, on this day, I will have to go up those steps, turn left, go through the door, and enter the room – the room with 1,000 demons. Lately, however, those demons seem to accompany me wherever I go – they don't just stay in that room.

Oh, there are times when I can stuff them into some corner of my being – times when I can pretend they do not exist. Yet again, though, I am reminded that silence is not golden; maybe ignorance truly *is* bliss.

So, I'll go into that room. I'll use this story as my crutch. I'll stammer around trying to avoid the unavoidable – wishing it would go away – and realizing (again) that the very unanswered wish is proof that it must be true.

I don't want it to be true. Every bone, every muscle, every tendon, every ligament, every part of my being wants it not to be true. I guess that most of all my soul wants it not to be true. And, if it weren't true, I could grant that wish.

Since I can't grant that wish, it must be true.

It's a long way off right now – "the truth shall make you free." Right now the truth drags me down. It rips my guts out and utterly obliterates my foundation. For, if it is true (and it must be…), then my existence has been built upon false hopes. If it is true, then I am not who or what I had thought I was.

What is this damned truth that I cannot say out loud to her? I must say it out loud; I must acknowledge it as true. So, here goes: "My grandfather raped me."

I will say it again so I can hear it. "My grandfather raped me."

I will never be the same.

Cognitively I know that my physical being is still made up of the same molecules. My body still looks the same. I still have the same family, the same job, the same house.

I am not the same. I do not have the same past. So, some part of me has lied to other parts of me.

These were not/are not malicious lies. These lies are the product of a bright, creative little girl who did the very best she could to get through the repeated rapes – physical and spiritual ones. The thrusting, thrusting, thrusting so he could climax. I had to lie to myself to survive.

And, somehow, I have chosen now to tell myself the truth.

I know what she will say. She will say that I know me best – that I'll know when I'm ready for the truth. About a month ago, she suggested I might want some medication to help see me through. That was a tense time in my life. I began taking Paxil.

This last week has been hell. It took all the energy I could muster simply to make it through the day. Finally I crashed Saturday. I wanted to exist no longer. Even so, I had to keep existing for my kids. If it is this bad *with* the Paxil, I dread to think how bad it might have been *without* it.

I even called her at home Saturday. I probably shouldn't have done that. I needed to hear her voice. I don't want to burden her.

I want to go away. I want it not to be true. I want to wake up from this nightmare I have constructed for myself. Even so, the world keeps spinning on its axis, and I must deal with the truth: my grandfather raped me.

My grandfather raped me.

Four words – and I'm an empty shell. Who am I? Where did I come from? How can I reconcile this truth with the truth of what I've always believed about a loving God? How can Garth love a liar?

I want to get away. I want it not to be true.

It is true.

My grandfather raped me.

Where do I go from here?

How do I go from here?

"Hi! How are you today? Shall we go up?"

Help me.

Help me face the truth.

Help me grieve.

Help me hurt.

Help me heal.

Help me.

Please help me.

That's some awful stuff to slog through. Maggie likened it to a room with 1,000 demons. She volunteered to walk beside me, to guide me, to hold my hand, and to be present with me as we navigated across that room. She was a pastoral counselor. I didn't really know what that meant; I simply knew that she was there for me, that she cared about me, and that she would be with me as long as I asked her to be.

After three years, I really thought I had dealt with it. I can see now that I had done as much work as I could at the time. It was a long drive to her office; each time we met, I was away from home for at least four hours. My children were growing up, and I wanted to be at home more. I was also tired. Looking at scary things really is exhausting. I scheduled a "last" appointment with her. It was a bittersweet. While I was relieved and proud to have made it to the point that I was ready to end my therapy, I was also sad that I would not see Maggie on a regular basis any longer. I wrote another story to help me through that last appointment.

It sounds so final: "one last time." I don't like to think of it as the end … as one last time she pops her head through the door with that positive and energetic "How are you!" and one last time we walk together up the stairs and through the door into the room.

The room. It's her office. She's the "Executive Director" so she has a nice big office. She's even gotten new furniture during the course of our time together. (The "rape of the couch" is an entire story unto itself – one that can be remembered with laughter now yet seemed so egregious at the time.) Her name is etched in wood on a nameplate on her desk, and there is a cross at one end of the nameplate. I have told you about the clocks. They're everywhere. Some days they've ticked quite slowly; others, the time has flown by.

I'll go into that office one last time. I'll take my same seat one last time. Everything will be the same. And nothing will be the same.

My name is the same, and my physical appearance hasn't changed all that much. I've been in and out of contacts, and I've had my hair dyed, and I've had some surgery (just a few days ago). All in all, though, I look basically the same.

Appearances can be very deceptive. Beyond my physical appearance and my fundamental belief in a benevolent, omnipotent God who sent his son to die for me, nothing is the same. I have worked hard to get to this point, and I am thrilled to be at this place and to be moving in a good direction. She has guided me through hell. (At times, I'm sure she felt as if I were dragging her through it, too, since I have focused my anger directly at her on more than one occasion.)

So, one last time up the stairs, through the door, and onto my seat. Through it all, I've basically kept my tears in check while in that room. I don't think I'll succeed this time.

One last time is so bittersweet. It is hard to explain the shared intimacy to an outsider. I trusted her with all my crap; she didn't violate that trust. It is hard to let that go.

Yet, there comes a time when it is right to move on. A parent does everything in his/her power to help the child grow to the point that the child can make it on his/her own. So, too, does a counselor seek to enable and/or empower the client to recognize the power, skills, and worth within his/herself.

I've found the power, the skills, the sense of self-worth. It is time for me to go.

And, I'm thrilled to have reached this place.

And, I'm heartbroken to let go.

Even now, almost seven years later, I'm near tears as I remember that last appointment with Maggie. I was ready to go, but it was not easy to leave that last appointment. I did, though.

Thank you, Maggie, for your investment in me. I'm a better person for having walked with you.

Chapter 4: The Move and 9/11
2001

My last appointment with Maggie was in May of 2000. In September, my husband was invited to apply for a job in the Washington, DC area. I wanted to be supportive, but the thought of leaving two tenured positions was scary to me. I encouraged him to apply, but I wasn't sure he'd want to take the job if it were offered.

He was selected as one of three finalists for the position, and he interviewed in late February of 2001. He liked what he heard at the interview, and the choices that the administration was making at our current jobs were becoming more and more frustrating. Garth was selected as the top candidate and offered the job within a week of his interview. We talked about the possibility and prayed for guidance as we made our decision. In the final analysis, it seemed like the right thing to do, so he accepted the new position. We were going to move from the rural south to our nation's capital.

Our daughter, Zoë, was in fourth grade at the time. She was devastated when we told her that we would be moving over the summer. Watching her mourn stirred up feelings of fear and sadness in my inner child. If my daughter was so affected by this move, then how much more was I hurt by my grandfather's repeated violations of my soul? It was a different take on the abuse I experienced, but I ignored it and tried to help my son, Zeb, and daughter feel safe amidst the move.

We closed on our new house on July 10, 2001. My husband went to work every day, and I stayed home with the Zoë and Zeb and tried to unpack. I was sad and lonely, but I did not allow myself to mourn during the move. I thought I needed to take care of my children.

They started school on September 4, 2001. They were both in the same elementary school: Zoë was in fifth grade, and Zeb was in kindergarten. Since every child in kindergarten finds himself in a new place, Zeb adapted rather easily. The first week was harder for Zoë. By the weekend, she was complaining of a sore throat; she did not want to go to church Sunday morning. She didn't have any fever, and, when I looked at her throat, I couldn't see anything wrong with it. I figured she was just trying to avoid having to go to the new church, and Garth agreed. We made her go. She was still complaining after we got out of church, and she didn't want to go play. I hoped she wasn't coming down with something.

Since Monday was a busy day for me at work, Garth took the day off to take Zoë to the doctor. It turned out that she had strep throat. I felt really bad about having made her go to church. After taking antibiotics for one day, she still was not feeling quite right Tuesday; she wanted to stay home another day. I needed to teach one morning class, and then I could be at home for the rest of the day. Zoë assured us that she would be okay at home alone for a few hours. I checked with a neighbor to make sure she would be around in case Zoë needed anything, and Garth and I decided that I would go in to teach my morning class and he would leave for work a little later than usual. That would mean that Zoë would be alone only for a couple of hours.

When I got off the Metro in DC, I heard people talking about a plane hitting the World Trade Center. Like many, I assumed that it was a small plane and the pilot had experienced medical problems, passed out, and lost control of the plane. When I got to my office, I tried to check it out on CNN.com, but I couldn't get the page to load. (I guess there was too much traffic, but I didn't know that at the time.) I needed to get ready for class, so I moved on to other things.

Garth called me when he got to his office. I assumed that he was calling to find out whether I had talked to Zoë or not. Instead, he told me to go home at once. I told him that he was being overprotective and assured him that Zoë would be fine until I got home after my class. I'll never forget his reply: "They've hit New York, and they're coming to DC next. Go home."

I was very confused; I asked him what he meant. He explained to me that a second plane had hit the other tower. He was pretty sure it was some sort of attack and that he believed there would be an attack on DC soon. Then he pleaded with me to leave. I pointed out that I could be fired for dereliction of duties if I simply left. When he told me he didn't care if I was fired, I realized that he was truly concerned that I could be in harm's way in DC and that he didn't want Zoë to be home alone if and/or when an attack came. He was going to leave his office, too, and meet me at home. Zeb was at school.

Since I had taken the Metro in, I had to take the Metro home. As I headed out, there were many, many others streaming to the Metro station, too. By this time, unbeknownst to most of us, the Pentagon had been hit. Metro was stopping at the first station outside DC, offloading passengers, and sending trains back into the District to evacuate more people. The platform was jammed. Everyone was calm, but we didn't how long it might be before trains were running past the first station.

I knew that I could probably walk home from that station, but I realized that I didn't know *where* to walk. I had only traveled *under* the streets on the train; I had no idea how to get from that station to home above ground. So, I waited with many others.

Finally, trains started running beyond that station again. I'd never been on a car that was so tightly packed, and I'll probably never see one so full again. It was truly heartwarming to watch people doing their best to take care of each other. There was a woman with two young children in a double stroller. Her husband had flown up for a meeting, and she decided to join him. Not only was she dealing with her children; she also didn't know where her husband was, or when she might see him again. Folks rallied around her and cleared a spot on the train for her very large stroller. Normally seats are taken on a first-come, first-served basis. On this day, people tried to figure out who really needed a seat and then did their best to see that they got one.

I had no idea that the attacks were being shown on live television. Fortunately, when we got home, we found Zoë watching game shows, blissfully unaware of what was transpiring just a few miles away. We could see wisps of smoke from the fire at the Pentagon from our front steps.

The rest of that week was a blur. Garth and I wondered whether we had made the right choice to move. I worried about our property values since much of our savings was tied up in our house. (That was a necessity due to the very high housing costs up here.)

9/11 stirred up feelings of that lost inner child again. I squashed them back down and tried to help my children adjust to the move and the knowledge that terrorists had flown planes into buildings – one of them being the Pentagon, which is less than five miles from our house as the crow flies.

Zeb was a typical kindergartener; he made good friends quickly and felt like he fit in. Fortunately, there were three girls in the fifth grade who welcomed Zoë into the fold; gradually she felt accepted. They became quite the foursome.

Neither Zoë nor Zeb wanted to get on a plane to fly south for Christmas, so we decided to take the train. We found a "family" sleeper car and made reservations for a twenty-seven hour train ride. It was a new thing for all of us, so it was exciting to hop on the train. We boarded around 7 p.m., got things settled in our cabin, and ventured down to the dining car for supper. The food was good, the servers were quite congenial, and we met another family traveling with children about the ages of ours. When we got back to our cabin, the kids surprised us with a Christmas tree and Advent wreath they had made using construction paper; it was so sweet. It felt like things were finally settling down after the move and the upheaval of 9/11.

When it was time for bed, the kids climbed up on the top bunk. Zeb was on the inside of the bed and put his head toward one end of the cabin; Zoë was on the outside with her head toward the other end. That seemed to work pretty well, and both kids fell asleep. Garth and I shared the lower bed; it was almost as wide as a double bed and about one inch longer than Garth is tall. I was on the inside with him on the outside. In theory, it was going to be cozy and safe with him protecting me from whatever might come into the room. I closed my eyes and tried to get some sleep.

Boom!

I can't explain it, but being crowded in that bed with my husband's body "blocking" my way out made me feel like I was back in the trailer with my grandfather with his body blocking any escape. I tried to tell myself that it was my husband who loved me and would take care of me, but this inner voice kept telling me that it was *not* a good thing and I had to get out!

I managed to get about two hours of fitful sleep, and I tried to ignore the fact that such scary thoughts had invaded my mind so quickly and unexpectedly. After all, I had worked really hard with Maggie; I had gotten "past" all of the awfulness that my grandfather had dished out.

The time with our respective families was uneventful. It was good to be back with them so they could see for themselves that we really had survived 9/11 and were adjusting to our new lives. Then it was time to get back on the train for the trip north.

The return trip left early in the morning. We had all day in our cabin reading new books, playing card games, working puzzles. Amtrak even showed movies on the small video terminal in the room. The food was good; the kids liked staying in the cabin when we went to eat, and the servers were happy to pack up their food for them to have in the room.

Darkness fell. The train lumbered on; the motion can be calming like watching ocean waves meet the shore time and time again. It was New Year's Eve, and we saw fireworks out our window. That was fun. Finally it was time to go to bed. The kids got settled in. I was suddenly very nervous about going to bed, but I didn't want to let Garth know. It seemed so silly to be afraid of lying down next to him. I tried to remind myself that it was Garth who loved me and cared for me and would protect me. I delayed climbing in for as long as I felt like I could. Finally I had to get into the lower bunk.

I lay there with my eyes wide open; I hoped that the scary feelings might not come as long as I didn't close my eyes. The train lurched (as trains do), and my husband, who was sleeping, rolled into me.

Suddenly I *was* that little girl trapped in the trailer. His body was blocking any access to a safe exit, and he was going to hurt me. I didn't want to be there, but it felt like there was no way out. I didn't want to bother Garth because I felt so stupid and inadequate for not being able to distinguish between the present reality that I was safe in a cramped bed on a train and my sense of urgency about what I imagined was happening. How could I tell him that I felt like he was my grandfather who was about to suffocate and gag me? I couldn't, and I didn't.

We got home. I was exhausted, and I knew that I needed help. I hated that I couldn't shake those feelings on the train, but Maggie had been so good and helpful that I believed every therapist would be equally as good and helpful.

I floundered for several months trying to figure out what to do. It was time for my annual gynecological exam, so I had to find a physician. By sheer accident – or divine providence – I stumbled into a wonderful practice, a single female physician who had left a larger practice because she felt like she wasn't getting enough time with her patients. Garth accompanied me to my first visit to provide moral support.

After I had gotten so angry with Maggie for asking, "Always?" she had suggested that I might to ask my physician about antidepressants. I didn't want to do that because I didn't want to be "so bad off" that I needed medications to help me; I didn't want the stigma of having to take an antidepressant. But, Maggie encouraged me, and, when I asked my doctor about it, she also thought it was a good idea. I had quit taking them before my final session with Maggie.

Now I was in a new town with a new physician and old fears. I asked her about antidepressants; her response was very affirming. She opined that we ought to add them to the water supply because she believed almost everyone could benefit from them. So, I started taking medication again. I felt a bit like a failure for needing it.

I accepted that I needed to find a therapist again. Too much had happened since my last visit with Maggie; I knew I had still had work to do. I couldn't figure out the best way to go about finding the right therapist in a new town. I didn't want to go around telling my friends that my grandfather had done unimaginably horrible things to me when I was younger; I was afraid that would clue them into how awful I truly was. I ran across a book by a therapist who specializes in working with survivors of childhood sexual abuse. The bio on the back flap told of her private practice. I decided to contact the author to see if she could recommend any therapists near me.

I couldn't find the courage to call her and say – out loud – that my grandfather had done these awful things to me. Instead I wrote a letter and sent it to an address I had found by Googling her name. She called me several days later and gave me the names of several therapists whom she knew worked with survivors of childhood sexual abuse in my area. I looked at those names for a couple of weeks before finding the courage to call one of them.

I called Dottie. She had an opening, so I made an appointment to meet with her.

Chapter 5: Not the Right Fit
March, 2002 – May, 2004

My first impression of Dottie was that she was the anti-Maggie. I was basing that on physical appearances only. Maggie was a petite, blue-eyed blond with short hair; Dottie was taller, with dark eyes and long, dark hair. Maggie was licensed as an LPC (Licensed Professional Counselor) and an LMFT (Licensed Marriage and Family Therapist), and she practiced at a pastoral counseling center. On the other hand, Dottie was part of a private practice, and was licensed as an LCSW (Licensed Clinical Social Worker). Before meeting with Dottie, I had tried to determine the differences among the various licenses. What I gleaned from my research was that there were slight differences in the training and education for those who held the various licenses and that a therapist with any of the various licenses was equally as likely to be good at talk therapy as one who held a different license. So, I didn't think much of the distinction between Maggie, the LPC/LMFT, and Dottie, the LCSW.

Since the author had recommended Dottie after I explained my history to her and since Dottie's office was within walking distance of my own office, I assumed that Dottie was the right therapist for me. I thought that it was divine guidance that had led me to the book, helped me find the author's address, and caused her to call me – a total stranger – back after she received my letter. The friend who recommended Maggie to me told me that he had worked with several therapists and Maggie was the best he had ever seen, so, when I didn't feel an immediate connection to Dottie, I thought that having worked with the best first simply made all other therapists pale by comparison.

There were things that bothered me, but I didn't trust myself to be able to determine whether Dottie was right for me or not. After all, Dottie did help me feel better about some things, and I was able to tell her about the awful things my grandfather had done and how I had felt in the bed on the train.

I had felt a connection with Maggie, and I didn't feel that same connection with Dottie. For example, I knew that Maggie's husband was a minister and they had two children – an older daughter and a younger son. I also had an older daughter and a younger son, and that helped me feel connected. At the time, I didn't fully understand the importance – at least for me – of feeling connected to my therapist.

Dottie carefully guarded any personal information; she did so with such a passion that I began to wonder if Maggie had somehow violated a professional code of conduct. It was not clear to me whether Dottie was married or not, straight or gay, or spiritual or not. It did leak out that she had a daughter about my son's age. That was the sum total of what I knew about her beyond where her office was located, what her fees were, her voicemail number, and who was covering her calls when she was out of pocket.

I had asked Maggie for a hug one day, and she was happy to oblige. When I mentioned to Dottie that I wanted a hug, she took an entire session asking me to explain *why* I wanted the hug. That was very confusing for me. Once again I feared that Maggie had violated a professional code. I never told Dottie that Maggie had hugged me because I was afraid that I'd get Maggie in trouble. The truth is, for me, talking about the abuse I experienced in my childhood awakens feelings of fear, loneliness, and sadness in my inner child, and that inner child wants to feel a hug to know that she will be okay.

Dottie's office was close to mine. I'd walk over and go in. Since there was no receptionist, there was a coded lock on the door. Clients were given the code to punch in so they could access the waiting area if they arrived early for an appointment. Several times, I got there before Dottie and found that the door wouldn't open after I had punched in the code. That made me feel like I wasn't welcome there; the little girl within felt abandoned. After that happened the third time, I asked Dottie why she was running late. She replied that she had been caught in traffic. Well, anyone who has experienced the frustrations of driving on the Capital

Beltway, 66, 270, 295, 395, the GW Parkway, or the BW Parkway can completely understand being caught in traffic. I accepted that as a reasonable excuse.

Somehow I found out that her practice was *not* Dottie's primary job; I learned that she worked for one of the local county governments in her capacity as an LCSW. To this day, I don't really know what she did there; I simply know that I tired of being locked out and having to wait for her in the hall because she was stuck in traffic somewhere.

When I asked if we needed to adjust our appointment time, she told me that we did not and promised not to be late again. A few weeks later, something came up, and she asked me to move my appointment just for that week to a different day. I was happy to do so. When I arrived on the different day, I once again found myself locked out. Well, that made me feel like I was an abandoned little girl, and I could hear my grandfather reminding me that nobody cared about me. I felt like Dottie didn't care about me. I waited and waited. She was much later than usual. Finally, I grew tired of waiting and left.

It turns out that her child had become ill and needed to see the doctor. I completely understood. What I could *not* understand was why she didn't call my cell phone to let me know. She told me she didn't have a cell phone. I asked whether she had access to a phone at the doctor's office; her response was evasive. I began to feel as though Dottie's priorities were her family first (which is completely defensible), her "real" job next, with her clients at her practice coming in a distant third. I asked Dottie if her practice was merely a hobby. She assured me that it was not.

I couldn't tell whether I was making progress or not. Garth knew I needed to be seeing *somebody*, and he knew it had been hard for me to find Dottie. Neither of us wanted to go through a period of searching for a new therapist yet again. So I hung in there with Dottie.

Another of my frustrations with Dottie was the way she dealt with voicemail. I did not like having a call into her and then wonder about *when* she was going to respond. I asked her to tell me her policy. I didn't really care what it was, I just wanted to know what to expect. I told her that I would be happy with something as broad as, "I will return all voicemail messages by 10 p.m. every Thursday."

She told me that she simply could not do that because her life was too unpredictable. Well, that response upset me. I was coming to see her because I had endured awful things as a little kid. Part of me was *still* that little kid, and little kids crave predictability. I tried to explain it to her that way. She told me she understood what I was saying but that she simply couldn't make any promises as to when voicemail would be returned.

One day when she returned my voicemail, the message I heard was actually a message that another client had left her. Somehow she had forwarded that message to me. That caused me to wonder who might have heard some of my phone calls to her.

By March of 2004, I was really frustrated with what I perceived to be the utter lack of predictability for her responses to her phone messages. Once again I brought it up. She assured me that she would always get back to me "as quickly as possible." I asked her what that meant, and she couldn't – or didn't – give me a straight answer. I told her that this was really a problem for me and was so important to me that it could be a deal breaker. I didn't want to have to find a new therapist, so I begged her to come up with some policy. I told her I didn't care if it was that she would return calls once a week – I wanted predictability. Again she told me that she simply could not do that; she promised she would do better.

I called one day in May of 2004. Her greeting noted that she was out of town and she would return all messages Monday. I was so happy to have a day that I knew meant a response was coming.

Monday came. No response by noon. Still no response by 5 p.m. Still no response by 9 p.m. I went to bed late that night still having received no response. I didn't understand, and I felt abandoned.

Tuesday she called while I was in class and left me a message. In her message to me, she told me that she had just been too busy Monday to return calls.

That was the final straw. I pointed out that *I* had not asked her to call me back Monday – instead *she* was the one who had said she would return calls then. Her response felt far more defensive than apologetic.

I walked out of her office for the last time. Before I left, I told her that I would never be back. I left her a message telling her I was never coming back. I sent a letter so she would have it in writing. I never saw Dottie again.

I don't know why it was so hard to leave Dottie. Certainly I had been frustrated with her for over a year, and I never felt a connection to her. I probably should have extricated myself from that situation far earlier. I simply didn't want to deal with trying to find a new therapist again.

I tried to convince myself that I no longer needed therapy, but I knew that I still had things I needed to examine, question, and understand. I wanted to find a better match, so I tried to figure out what the differences were between Maggie and Dottie. I wanted another Maggie, not another Dottie. I didn't know whether the distinction between the LPC/LMFT and LCSW was crucial. I did some more research and came to believe that the real distinction was that between *therapy* and *pastoral counseling*. I hoped that all I needed to do was find a pastoral counselor.

I got on my computer and Googled "pastoral counseling" and Washington, DC. Several hits appeared. After browsing the various websites, I settled on a practice that had offices that were convenient to my house or easily accessible from my office. The next step was to select from among the names. I read the bios and prayed about it. I settled on three and called each one's voicemail. I explained a little about my background and asked if I could come see them.

It was the summer – late June. I think I called on a Friday. So, I didn't hear anything for a few days. I typed letters to each one of the people I had called and was about to mail them when my phone rang. It was Carol, and she had gotten my message and wanted to give me a call back. Yes, she could meet with me. We set up an appointment for the following Wednesday. I prepared a lengthy letter hoping to avoid the problems I had experienced with Dottie.

Little did I know that I was to meet someone whose style is a really good fit for what I needed and who is a wonderful pastor and counselor. I have always believed that God is active in our daily lives. We don't always see what he does, but he is always working on our behalf. I believe that either Carol was not ready for me in March of 2004 or I was not ready for her. If I had found a "good" fit with Dottie then, I wouldn't have walked away, and I never would have met Carol.

Romans 8:28 reminds us that "God causes all things to work together for good for those who love God and are called according to His purpose." When I was becoming so frustrated with Dottie, I had no idea that I was about to be so blessed by Carol.

Chapter 6: Finding Carol
July – September, 2004

Maggie is older than I, and Dottie is about my age. When I met Carol for the first time, I was struck by how young she was. Like Maggie, she has blond hair and blue eyes; like Maggie, she works out of a pastoral counseling center. She is not an LPC, an LMFT, or an LCSW: she is an ordained minister, The Reverend Carol Froya. I had prepared a lengthy written document detailing my history that closed with five questions I wanted to ask her. Here are parts of it.

It is probably strange that I am writing to you when I haven't even met you yet. I suppose I'm trying to show you most of my "warts" during our first meeting. That way, you'll see them sooner, and you can know whether or not you can work with me sooner, and I can "cut my losses" (as it were) if you decide you can't work with me.

Let me tell you about my most recent past and how I wound up here in this room with you. Of course, that requires me telling you a bit about my farther ago past.

I was sexually and emotionally abused by my mother's father from when I was about two years old until his death about three months after my sixteenth birthday. (I suppose all sexual abuse can be defined as "emotional" in some way.) He told me I was bad ... really bad ... and, if anyone else found out how bad I was, it would be awful for me. Furthermore, he told me he was really smart ... smart enough to help me hide how bad I was as long as I did what he told me to do. So, I was bad, and he was smart enough (and kind enough) to help me hide my badness.

I was also, for lack of a better term, a "sex object" for the older boy (Kendrick) who lived next door. He "initiated" me into his secret club and used me whenever his teenage hormones kicked in. All my life I have remembered Kendrick and at least some of the things he did to me.

*[*I've omitted much of what I wrote in the middle of this letter.*

It's details I've given earlier in this book.]*

One year later (spring of 2001), my husband was offered a job in the DC area. We had both earned tenure. We were living in my dream house. We never thought we would leave ... until the administration started doing some stupid things and Garth got the job offer. I really didn't want to leave the security of the "known" to face the unknown ... however, there was the lure of being farther away from my parents. ☺ Plus, God kept sending little (or gigantic) signs that this was what we were supposed to be doing.

First, I tried to point out (to God) that I didn't have a job up here and that we probably couldn't afford to live up here if I didn't get a job ... no problem. My dean talked to the dean at a school up here, and I got a contact. I talked with my department at up here in March ... they didn't currently have any openings, but I could certainly stop by to say "hello" when we were up here over spring break. Well, by spring break, someone had quit unexpectedly ... and I had an offer for a one-year position.

So, next I pointed to the "housing" issue ... how could we ever sell our house and find one in DC. Oh ye of little faith ... that's really not a problem ... our daughter ended up selling our house to one of her classmates (it's a longer story), and we came up here and found our house in three days ... thanks to some friends we had in Reston who recommended a good real estate agent ... of course all of that was with Divine guidance.

I have always believed that God is very active in our day-to-day lives. I believe that He has had a hand in bringing me here. I'm not sure what will happen; I am sure that something will work out. I do have a list of questions for you now that I've laid out my past. Maybe you can answer them if you're not too turned off by this tome ...

1. Have you worked with incest survivors? If so, approximately how many?

2. What do you think it means that I can't get "the facts" all straight in my mind? (By that I mean I don't have "clear" and/or

"complete" details ... just the sense that I've got it right ... and, I've checked with my sisters, and they offer affirmation.)

3. What is your policy on returning phone calls? (This is very important to me ... I don't have to know you'll return my call in X hours ... I do want to know a "drop dead" time by which I can absolutely expect to have my calls returned ... and, if that is once a week, that's okay. This is what finally led me to terminate my relationship with Dottie ... the little girl part of me wants predictability there.)

4. What does "the little girl part of me" mean to you? (Is it okay that I refer to a "little girl part"?)

5. What does "pastoral counseling" mean to you?

Carol was happy to answer those questions, and I was glad to hear her responses. Almost immediately, I sensed a connection to her – even during that first scary appointment. Carol was trained in CBT (cognitive behavioral therapy). Once Maggie had jokingly warned me to "watch out" for "CBT-ers" because she thought they might focus too much on ready-made exercises and not enough on meeting clients where they were. My feeling of being connected to Carol outweighed Maggie's expressed concerns about CBT-trained therapists. I was ready to go to work.

After a first session with a client, Carol often asks the client to find a favorite Psalm. When I received that assignment, I found one and gave her much more at our next meeting.

As I told you, I tend to write. It is a good form of reflection for me. As I reflect on our conversation yesterday, I have a few (more?) questions/comments.

First, at times it seemed like you were referring to the fall as being a "long way off." That makes me wonder how long you think therapy should last. I tend to go back and forth on this myself. However, I always return to thinking, "hey, he did things to me for 13 years, so I'm not going to feel too bad about myself if I want to be in therapy for 13 years – or for 26 – or for 39." I have gracefully ended therapy when I thought I was ready (with Maggie) and abruptly ended a therapeutic relationship that didn't feel right, even though I didn't think it was time to stop exploring. So, I think I'll be able to discern when it is time to move on whether to another therapist or simply with life. I want to make sure that you don't view this as a "short-term" treatment plan. I want to know that I can keep coming as long as I feel the need to do so. (Of course, at the same time, I understand that no one can make "permanent" guarantees ... you could move away after you complete your doctorate, for example.)

Second, I really feel like what I need to do now is grieve for that little girl who was treated so badly. And, I'm not very good at that. I don't like to cry in front of others, and some part of me thinks that this is all in the past so I should just get on with it. I guess I need permission to grieve; I need to know that it isn't stupid or weak. (I spent the vast majority of my "formational" years hearing my grandfather tell me how awful I was. That is hard to discount.)

I really appreciate your giving me your cell phone number. I hope I don't ever feel the need to use it. I think part of the deeper meaning surrounding the whole phone call issue with Dottie was the feeling of not being "good enough" to merit a better way to reach her if things went to hell in a hand-basket. I appreciate your trusting me with that number; I appreciate being "good enough" to get it.

(Maybe I write so I can cry when I'm alone ... it's safer that way, and I don't look weak or stupid to others. Right now Garth has taken Zeb over to some friends' house (twins) to play, and Zoë is still in bed. (She is now a teenager!))

On to the Psalms – one important thing to me as I peruse scripture is the particular translation. These days I tend to favor the New Living (which, as you know, was translated phrase by phrase for meaning from the original texts – unlike the Living Bible which was paraphrased from other English translations) and *The Message*. The New Living happens to be by the computer right now, so I'll look at it first. Then I'll get *The Message* and compare.

As I flip through, I can't help but hear the music I have sung to so many of the Psalms. For example, Psalm 24: Lift up your heads, O ye gates ... Who is the King of glory? Who is the King of glory? The Lord strong and mighty – a great choral piece or Psalm 27 "The Lord is my light and my salvation – whom then shall I fear? Whom shall I fear?" (No, neither of those is the New Living translation; rather, it is most likely some variant of the King James. I'm just remembering singing them.) There is "He watching over Israel slumbers not nor sleeps" – a lush and beautiful Mendelssohn (perhaps from *Elijah*). I can't remember if that is a Psalm or not, but it seems like one. Psalm 47 "Come, everyone, and clap your hands for joy! ... God has ascended with a mighty shout." Then there's Rutter's *Requiem* and Psalm 130: "Out of the deep, have I called unto you, O Lord. Lord, hear my prayer." (continuing from the New Living) "Lord, if you kept a record of our sins, who, O Lord, could ever survive? But you offer forgiveness that we might learn to fear you. ... O Israel, hope in the Lord; for with the Lord there is unfailing love and an overflowing supply of salvation. He himself will free Israel from every kind of sin." Of course Psalm 150: "Praise ye the Lord! Praise God in his sanctuary! Praise him for his mighty works! Praise hymn with the loud sounding trumpet! Praise him with the lyre and harp! Let everything that hath breath praise the Lord. Praise ye the Lord!"

So, I flipped through the first thirty or so, and then to the last twenty or so ... **a** favorite ... hmmm ... Let me go get *The Message* ... the more I hear the Rutter in my head, the more I have to go with Psalm 130 for now; Here's Rutter's translation[8]:

> "Out of the deep have I called unto Thee, O Lord: Lord, hear my voice.
> O let Thine ears consider well the voice of my complaint.
> If Thou, Lord, wilt be extreme to mark what is done amiss, O Lord, who may abide it?
> For there is mercy with Thee: therefore shalt Thou be feared.
> I look for the Lord; my soul doth wait for Him: in His word is my trust.
> My soul fleeth unto the Lord; before the morning watch, I say, before the morning watch.
> O Israel, trust in the Lord, for with the Lord there is mercy: and with Him is plenteous redemption.
> And He shall redeem Israel from all His sins."

---

[8] This is from John Rutter's *Requiem* which he composed in 1985.

Months later Carol pointed out to me that I had selected the Psalm that says, "Out of the deep, have I called unto, O Lord." I didn't see it at the time, but I *was* calling out of the depths of fear and terror.

I was baptized when I was ten years old in an attempt to make him stop doing all those horrible things he was doing to me. The hymn said that I would be "washed whiter than snow." In my young mind, I reasoned that being baptized would make me not be so terribly, awfully bad. Then, I figured that, if I were no longer terribly, awfully bad, I wouldn't need him to protect me anymore. So he would quit doing all those things to me.

My grandfather knew what I was doing. He told me that it wouldn't work because I was such a terrible, awful, bad person that God didn't want me. Sure enough, my grandfather could see that I was still bad – even after having been baptized. I wasn't washed whiter than snow.

I knew that as the truth, and I didn't want Carol to find out. I really felt a connection to her; she told me that she believed in me – that she saw good things for me. That was so foreign. Here was an ordained minister – someone with divine insight – who thought I was good. She thought that what I want mattered. She told me that she cared if it hurt. I loved hearing those things, and I was grateful that she was convinced that they were true. In the meantime, I kept hearing what a bad person I was and that she would eventually figure that out. When I told Carol that I was scared she was going to figure out how bad I really was, she told me that she didn't agree with the "tapes" that he had put there. She said the tapes were lies and she believed that one day I would no longer believe them.

Wow. That was a new concept: the "tapes" were lies that he put there. She didn't believe that I was a terrible, awful, bad person. She is smart; in fact, she is working on her Ph.D. She is also an ordained minister. So, she has "book smarts," common sense, and divine insight. With all those tools, she still didn't see anything bad in me. I kept waiting for the other shoe to drop.

In September, I finally found the courage to tell her about getting baptized but not being worthy of being washed whiter than snow. I told her that I wondered where God was all the times he was doing those things to me. And, I waited for her to tell me that she really had finally seen the truth about my badness.

She didn't say that. She told me that she believed in me and she was proud of me for saying things that were so hard to say.

Wow. I didn't know what to think. I wanted to believe her, and I was scared to hope too much because I still expected a day to come when she finally saw the truth. She consistently, patiently, persistently told me that she did not agree with the tapes, that the tapes were lies that he had put there, and that she saw really good things in my future. She left me great voicemail messages. Here's one from September, 2004. I had talked with her on a Friday afternoon, but I had been to scared to say what I really wanted to say. I called her voicemail and told her that I hadn't been able to say it. This is her response.

> Hey there, S. It's Carol. I picked up your message this morning that you had left Friday. I had some clients this morning, but I thought as long as I had a bit of a break I'd call back and see if I might be able to catch you or at least leave a message.
>
> I just wanted to say that I'm really sorry that you weren't able to say what you wanted to be able to say on Friday. Hopefully we'll have some time to talk about that tomorrow, too. [We were to meet the next day.]
>
> In way of reassuring you again, this is some hard stuff that you're getting into. At the same time, it is also a signal to me, both clinically and spiritually, that things are going in a direction that is productive. This is some hard stuff to look at and some stuff that had been squished down for a while. This is, I'm sure, no new information to you.

At the same time, in way of reassuring you, I believe in you. I believe that this is going to be a productive process for you and that there is some stuff worth taking a look at here.

So, you take care. You have my voice mail. As always, if you wanted to talk in between, my cell is …

See you tomorrow.

She wanted to help me say these really hard things because she knew that *I* wanted to say them. She never pressured me; she waited patiently and kept telling me that she believed in me, thought I was a good person, saw good things for me, and cared about what I thought.

I had been elected to a leadership role in my church. I felt like a hypocrite because I knew how bad I was; at the same time, I *did* try to do what a "good" person would do. I assumed they had put me in this position because they thought that I was the good person I pretended to be. In the summer and fall of 2004, our pastor went on sabbatical. I led the service to bless him as he departed, and I led the service to welcome him back when he returned. For the return service, I used circles as metaphors for his journey and ours. He was returning to us – completing the circle of his journey and our circle of fellowship. I wanted to remind us that we, the church, needed to be welcoming to all who came – ensuring our circle was big enough, inviting enough, and safe enough for any and all who wanted to join in. I invited Carol to that service, and she came. She and I started talking about circles, too.

In part, I felt a bit frustrated because it seemed like I kept returning to the same questions. It felt like I was going in a circle and not making any real progress. Carol assured me that she saw progress; she told me it was not unexpected – nor necessarily unusual – that I would ask the same questions again and again. She tried to explain the way the brain works to me. In essence, we have lots of brain cells that are connected to each other by neural pathways. She likened a young child's brain to a hill with fresh snow, and the neural pathways are established by "sledding" down the hill. It is easy to create paths on the fresh snow, but, as the paths become more and more established (by repeatedly sledding down them), it becomes harder and harder to create new paths.

Carol explained that my grandfather's lies had formed dysfunctional and incorrect pathways, and it was going to be hard to get the sled off those well-worn paths to create new ones. She did her best to reassure me that it was okay to ask the same question again and again – even if it felt like going around in circles; she told me that she was seeing progress. So, I kept on trying to put one foot in front of the other.

Sometimes I think we're too close to see our own progress.

Chapter 7: Circles
October, 2004 – October, 2006

October marks the end of one year and the beginning of the next for me; it's where my circle begins anew. In October of 2004, I turned 45. Every October 31st, I once again am reminded of the time my grandfather took me out trick-or-treating. That's an insidious cycle; Carol assures me that a Halloween will come when it's not as bad.

That awful night, we left his house and turned right to go down the hill. The darker yard (with the bush he hid behind when he dropped his pants and made me suck on his penis) was around the curve at the bottom of the hill. The house I live in now is at the end of a cul-de-sac at the top of a hill. Going trick-or-treating requires walking down the hill and going around the corner at the bottom. I just couldn't do that. I was grateful that Garth took Zeb trick-or-treating. As a middle-school student, Zoë thought she was too old to go trick-or-treating. Instead, she met up with some friends and walked around from house to house asking for candy. (Yes, it sounds a lot like trick-or-treating, but I'm told that it wasn't.)

I stayed home to greet any ghosts or goblins who might come around asking for candy. I also started working on the service that was to mark Bob's return from his sabbatical. I found myself contemplating circles. Here's what I wrote that Halloween night in anticipation of the Second Sunday in Advent and our pastor's return.

> Think of the many circles in our lives. Today, we celebrate the second Sunday of Advent, and we see before us the circular Advent Wreath which reminds us of the never-ending love of God: God loves us so much that he sent his only son to die in order to redeem us. From death comes everlasting life. Our liturgical year is circular: it begins anew every year on the first Sunday of Advent. Our calendar year begins on January 1st and ends on December 31st – which is followed again by January 1st. Every day the sun rises and sets, a cycle which goes on and on.

We have seen the ripples going out in circles when a stone is tossed into calm waters. At many weddings, we are reminded of the symbolism of the circular wedding ring representing continuous, endless love. The scriptures speak of God as Alpha and Omega – the beginning and the end. Even children's movies, such as *The Lion King*, tell of the circle of life.

Today, as we celebrate Bob's return from his sabbatical, we participate in the completion of a circle: Bob's return to the place from which he began his journey. We will also consider the many circles in our lives. As Bob was leaving, I used a poem by John Donne to remind each of us that we are all connected – that no man is an island. As he returns, I will use another poem by John Donne – a poem Donne wrote as he was leaving on trip himself.[9] The poet speaks of "just" circles. The prophet Isaiah also speaks of circles: a new branch will emerge from the stump of David's tree – new fruit from a dead root. John the Baptist is also looking for fresh fruit.[10] Where do we fit into these circles? Do our circles fit into these truths?

Circles seemed to be everywhere – especially the one I felt I was walking around over and over again with Carol. It felt like from week to week I would move from one topic to the next and *always* end up back where I started. For example, I would ask Carol where God was and why he hadn't intervened on my behalf. When I felt like I had a bit of a handle on that, I would ask why she was so convinced I was a good person when I knew myself to be bad. We would talk about that, and then I'd move on to how scary sex was for me sometimes. I might point out that I thought I was supposed to enjoy sex because it is a sacred intimacy we share with each other. That would lead me to ask, "Where was God when he was doing these terrible things to me?"

---

[9] The first poem to which I refer is "Meditation XVII: No Man Is an Island" by John Donne. The second is "Valediction: Forbidden Mourning," also by Donne.

[10] The scriptures for the Second Sunday in Advent that year included Isaiah 11:1 – 10 and Matthew 3:1 – 12.

There I was right back where I had begun. Carol tried to explain to me that I was finding new understandings each time I revisited a question. I wasn't entirely convinced, but I did believe I was making some progress. The good days seemed to come more often, and the bad days didn't seem as bad. Nevertheless, I was frustrated to be going in circles. They felt like this:

One night as I was explaining my frustrations to Garth, I referred to the circular path that I seemed to keep repeating. Garth told me about a math professor he had had once. I don't remember what the course was (Garth does), but the professor put a function on the board. The class figured out that it was circular, but the circles were ascending. The professor told them, "Yes! This is a 'car park.'"

I didn't understand why Garth had brought that up. It seemed to be totally unrelated to my frustrations of going over the same things again and again and again. Then he suggested that maybe my circles weren't simply circles – they could be the "car park" to which the professor referred. I was really confused because I had no idea what a "car park" was. Once Garth told me that his professor was British, I understood; he was referring to a parking garage. Suddenly it made sense! Maybe Carol really was right; maybe I was going around in circles in a parking garage. Each time I found myself at the same map coordinates, I was on a new level – gaining new understandings.

I couldn't wait to tell Carol about the "car park." She got it right away and agreed that it was a great way to describe what was happening.

As Carol and I talked about God's presence then and now, about whether or not I was good, about when Carol was going to figure out how bad I was, about when Carol was going to get tired of my phone calls, about whether or not I could ever learn to like sexual intimacy, I slowly came to believe her. She said she wasn't going to figure out how bad I was because she knew I wasn't bad; she also believed that one day I could also believe that I wasn't bad. She even suggested that I, in fact, was good. I had trouble believing that. I was still trapped in my circle.

In her church's organizational structure, Carol's "home" district is not the Washington, DC area. I began to worry that Carol was going to be placed somewhere in her home district when assignments were revisited (even though I knew that she had been assigned to DC every year since being ordained). I asked what would happen if they needed her back in her home district. She told me that those in charge knew her husband's job required him to be in DC, so moving back to her home district was really not an option.

It was April of 2006, and I really could see progress. I could agree that I probably was not a bad person. There were times when I believed that it really did matter what I wanted or thought. I had really good days. And, I was coming to a new understanding of where God had been during those awful moments. I asked again why she was so sure she wouldn't be assigned duties in her home district. She asked if I would be willing to share my thoughts with the people in charge of the assignments. This is what I wrote. In retrospect, I see that I learned a lot about myself simply by composing it. I don't know if I wrote the letter for Carol – or if I wrote it for myself.

Hello, Brothers and Sisters,

Thank you for taking the time to hear my thoughts. I want to tell you how profoundly Carol has affected my life and my faith journey. And, while I definitely want to sing Carol's praises, I hope you will see this letter in the larger context of highlighting the profound, and perhaps hidden, impacts of ordained ministers serving in roles beyond the traditional pulpit setting.

My experience began in my childhood: I was physically, sexually, and emotionally abused by my maternal grandfather. It began when I was two or three years old and continued until his death shortly after my sixteenth birthday. That's a long time, and the affects echo still today. On the surface, I have handled it pretty well. I've been married to a wonderful man for almost eighteen years, and we have two beautiful children. I earned a doctorate and hold a tenure-track faculty position a local university. I have served in a leadership role in my church for two years. I taught adult Sunday school classes from time to time and led seasonal devotions. I think that most people "looking" at me would think that I have a pretty good life.

The truth is that I've lived that last thirty years since my grandfather's death desperately trying to do the "right" things so that nobody would discover the truth about the terrible, awful, bad person I truly believed myself to be. That was the message that was pounded into my psyche over and over and over again for years and years – during my formative years. It stuck.

It stuck to the extent that I felt that I couldn't even risk telling my therapists how terrible I was for fear that they would abandon me. I worked with a pastoral counselor (LPC, LMFT) whose work focused on adults who had been molested as children for several years when I lived in the south. I thought I had addressed the bulk of the "stuff" I had to discuss, and I ended that relationship. We subsequently moved to the DC area in the summer of 2001. Suffice it to say that September 11, 2001, was a frightening day, and it touched that scared little girl inside. In the spring of 2002, I began working with a therapist (LCSW) who had been recommended to me by an author who has written several books on working with survivors of sexual abuse. That relationship lasted almost two years. In the end, it just didn't feel like I was getting what I needed.

I certainly didn't know what I needed, and I was tired of dealing with all the fallout. I stumbled across the website for Carol's practice and left a voice mail message for her and two other counselors who were listed as working with incest survivors. It felt like a long time passed; in reality, it was probably within the next couple of days that I got a call back from Carol. Since she was the first one to respond, I made an appointment to meet with her.

As I look back, I see God's active presence in the timing of those phone calls. Carol was the only ordained minister among the three people I contacted. At the time, whether or not she was ordained was completely and totally irrelevant. Yet, over the last two years – especially in the last few months – the fact that she is ordained has become such a blessing to me.

I grew up in church. My father was on the faculty at a religiously-affiliated university. He was a church organist for fifty years. It felt like we were at church any time the doors were open. We went to Sunday school and church Sunday mornings, training union and church Sunday evenings, and prayer meetings on Wednesday evenings. I walked the aisle, made my "public profession of faith," and was baptized when I was ten years old. I sang in children's choir then youth choir. I was active in the children's and youth programs. Upon graduating from high school, I went to the school where my father taught. I took the required Old Testament and New Testament classes (and made A's, of course!). I even took an extra Christian Ethics class. I stayed active in church. I worked at conference centers run by my denomination during my summer breaks: in the west for two years and then in the east for one year – at the eastern conference center, I was in a supervisory position and was hired, not through the conference center, but by personnel at the our denominational headquarters.

I met my husband singing in the church choir. I had completed my MBA and was working for a consulting firm; he was working toward his doctorate. We got married and were active in the church choir and on church council at the Methodist church where we lived.

I don't mean to wear you down with too many details. I'm trying to convey to you that I was coming from an extensive "church" background – the last twenty years in the Methodist church, the first twenty-six in a Baptist church. I was certainly "exposed" to all the "right things" in the church.

Yet, I was hiding a very big secret: I was such a terrible, awful, bad person that God himself had turned his back on me. I had to assume a cloak of righteousness for my children's and husband's sake.

And, still I thought very little of the fact that the counselor who called me back first was the ordained minister.

We speak of the "mystery" of faith ... of the resurrection. Maybe we should think of the words "mystery" and "miracle" as being interchangeable.

Over the course of the last twenty-one months, I have been able to tell Carol about my fears of being unworthy, about my failure to "get" Jesus, about my fears of being a hypocrite for appearing to be one thing while not really being that person. It has really come to a head over the last few weeks as I have faced progressively scarier and scarier things.

Suddenly, the veil was lifted. Suddenly, I "got" why God had led me to this wonderfully compassionate, incredibly patient, and steadfastly persistent instrument of his grace. It's not that other counselors couldn't have "gotten through" somehow; it's that the very fact that Carol is ordained was exactly and precisely what I needed. I've always believed in a God who is active in our lives. I very much believe that God led me to Carol and that God prepared Carol and me both for a shared experience of grace. I can't explain the mystery; I can only testify to the results.

Were Carol not ordained, I don't believe I could have made the same progress that I've made today. Now, I am willing to accept the premise that another ordained minister could have helped me in the same way. (The truth is that it is hard to imagine any one more able to meet me where I was than Carol; but, I have to acknowledge that God is far bigger than my limited understanding. If He had wanted to work it out another way, He certainly could have done so.)

The point I hope I've been able to articulate is this: there are people out there who need ordained ministers as counselors. It's simply not the same to seek counseling from one's church pastor. I couldn't have done that. For one, it would have blown my cover. Thank you for sharing your resources of ordained ministers with people like me. I was naked, and you helped clothe me. I was in prison, and you visited me. I was sick, and you comforted me. Thank you.

Carol was once again reappointed to the counseling center where she worked. (I am sure that my letter was *not* the primary reason for her reappointment to the DC area.) She continued to reassure me that she was going to be there for me for as long as I asked her to be. She told me that she was there, *not* because I was "good enough" or had done the "right things;" rather, she was there simply because I asked her to be.

Even though she is younger than I am, I came to think of Carol as my mom. I had also felt that same way about Maggie, but I had been too afraid to bring it up. I didn't know what the "rules" were about such things, and I didn't want to get in trouble. I finally was able to ask Carol to be my mom. She totally understood what I was asking and why; she also told me that I was not the first client to make that request. That made me feel better; sometimes I think we like knowing that we're not all that different from everybody else.

In two years I had made so much progress. I could see and feel it. Garth could see it, too. Oh, there were certainly still days when it would seem to come from nowhere. I wrote this in November of 2005.

Ugh! The enormity of it all hit me like a sledgehammer to the gut this morning. I guess that's the other side of the coin. If I'm going to tell the tapes to "fuck off!!!" and try to embrace that scared little girl, then I'm going to embrace *all* of that scared little girl. I had just dropped Zeb off at school and was driving away. *Boom!* There it was: ***My grandfather did all this shitty, crappy, terrible, awful, mean stuff to me.***

I think the process of coming to grips with knowing all of who you are and where you've been is incremental. Some of the steps are really, really small; other times, they're huge. I managed to navigate through that "boom" better than I had earlier. I suppose that was further evidence of progress.

I was doing better at handling the bumps along the way, but I was getting really tired of dealing with the tapes. I kept hearing that what I wanted didn't matter or that I was not this good person Carol believed me to be. I was tired of it, and I wanted to tell them, "***Shut the fuck up!!!***" I didn't really like that language. That is how St. Fu was born.

Every time I appealed to St. Fu, the tapes knew I was saying "Shut The Fuck Up!" I adopted St. Fu my patron saint, and I realized that he had been sitting on my desk watching over me for a long time. I had this obsidian paperweight that I called "the idol." I received it after my grandmother's death; in fact it had belonged to my grandfather before he died. That was sweet justice; St. Fu had been with him telling him (and the tapes) to shut up long before I knew he was there.

I could see progress and was feeling good. I likened it to growing up. I understand that some researchers posit that part of the person is "frozen" at the age the abuse began. If that's right (and it seems to fit what I know), then growing up is a good analogy. I was indeed growing up, and I wrote these goals down in late 2005:

1. Keep the tapes at bay with the goal of finally quieting them altogether.
2. Believe in myself as much as other people do.

3. Find a satisfactory answer to that little girl's question: "Why didn't God make him stop?"

4. Earn that little girl's trust.

5. Enjoy sex.

When I showed them to Carol, she liked these goals and commented that I might not have been able to believe that the second one was even possible when I first came to see her. I was making progress, indeed.

Chapter 8: I'm Good!
November, 2006 – January, 2007

I navigated another Halloween successfully. It did seem to be getting easier each year. Zoë was a sophomore in high school, and Zeb was in fifth grade. I felt like I was growing up with them. However, I was still frustrated from time to time because it felt like the other shoe would drop each time I thought I had made some really good progress. Carol told me that those times were like the charges that hadn't gone off during a fireworks show. The technicians had to set them off *after* the big finale to keep people from getting hurt if they exploded unexpectedly. She also assured me that those times would become less invasive. That helped me feel better. I was growing up, and I could see that things really were getting better. I wrote the following in November, 2006.

This whole "growing up" thing is bittersweet. I'm glad to feel better about navigating things on my own, and I miss the security of knowing you are there. I *know* that you haven't gone anywhere; I think I'm the one who is stepping out. I don't quite know how to say it. You're still there, and you're still my mommy. I know that I can call you any time I want to or need to call. I think before when I wouldn't call, it was because I didn't want to bother you. Now when I don't call, it's because I _____ … and this is where I just don't know how to put it. I feel different.

And, even saying "I feel different" feels like a déjà vu. There's that whole circle thing: I'm back in the spot where I claim that I feel different once again. This time, I really *do* think I've got it. I hope I'm not like Charlie Brown trying to kick the football, only to have Lucy yank it back yet again. And, Charlie Brown still hoped that the *next* time would be the time she wouldn't yank it away. So, I'm hoping that this will be the time that I won't have to face any more fireworks. Oh, I suspect there will always be times when I "see" or feel something new. I had some really bad shit happen to me, and I suspect there might always be a scar. The scar doesn't have to cripple me.

I hardly ever hear the tapes these days, and it's rare when I think about killing myself. Those tapes ... he put them there by telling me over and over and over and over and over and over and over and over and over and over and over and over and over again and again and again what a terrible, awful, bad person I was. Well, I think that maybe _he_ was the more terrible, more awful, and worse of the two of us. He did truly horrible, horrendous, horrific, terrible, bad, atrocious, repulsive, and awful things to me. Just because he did those things to me ... just because he told me that _I_ was the bad one ... just because he said so, doesn't make it so. He was wrong. He was wrong to do those things to me, and he was wrong to tell me how terrible, awful, and bad I was. He was wrong. Even his little idol knows it ... it's been shouting "Shut the fuck up!!" all these years, and I didn't know it. Besides "shut the fuck up!!" I wish somebody could/would tell him how badly he treated me.

I had reached a point where I could consider that I might be a good person without dismissing the notion as completely unfathomable. There were even moments when I almost believed it. There were times when I felt so _good_. When a bad day came, I had learned that it was okay to reach out for help. I had been reluctant to share the bad days with Garth or Carol because I was afraid they would grow weary of me and my bad days. Once I was able to see myself as something other than a terrible awful bad person, I could begin to wrap my head around the ideas that (1) they really wanted to be there for me and (2) they weren't going to abandon me just because I had another bad day.

As I've already noted, the bad days also came less often. I don't know if it was because I had learned to reach out for help on the bad days, was beginning to believe that a bad day didn't mean I had done something "wrong" or hadn't done something "right," or was able to see that the bad days simply weren't as bad; whatever it was, I was doing great.

January 26, 2007: thirty-one years after his death. I had told my sisters that he had done awful things to me, but I had never given them any specifics. I realized that I was trying to protect them from the gory details, and I knew I wanted to tell them some of the details because I didn't wanted some more help carrying them. I called Mary; we talked for over an hour. I told her some of the awful details. While it was exhausting, it also felt like the *right* thing to do.

Mary wasn't disgusted; she simply listened, shared my pain, and offered her support in whatever way I needed it. It was also an illuminating conversation for me. Since I had always *known* what a terrible, awful, bad person I was, I had always assumed that Cheryl and Mary put up with me out of some familial obligation. I was stunned to hear that they *loved* me, that they had cried together and prayed for me every night as I went through all the tests and surgery when my kidney was removed, and that they would have beaten him up – or worse – if they had only know what he was doing to me.

Wow. These were new concepts for me: my sisters really did love me, and they wanted to be there for me. I had called Mary on Saturday. On Wednesday, I received a handwritten card from her that read: *Thank you for "letting me come in" to your dark place. It's much easier to travel through scary places if someone who loves you is by your side. I am honored to walk with you every step of the way.* She closed with: *I love you, Baby Sister!* Then she added a note: *"Hopefully goes without saying – call <u>anytime</u>."*

I was so touched. Not only had she spent time with me Saturday, she had also taken more time to send me a card. I called her to thank her for the card, and she told me that she selected it because it was the right size for me to tuck into my purse so I could look at it whenever I needed to be reminded that she was there.

Thursday I received a card from Cheryl. She had made minor changes to a *Precious Moments* card so that it read:

> When you need
>> Someone to listen *& believe,*
> When you need
>> Someone to care,

When you need
>Someone to love you,
>A *sister*

>>*Was* always there
>>Is always there,
>>*& always will be there!*

A *sister* like you is a true blessing!

She closed: *Much love, Cheryl.* Then she added Galatians 6:2: "Carry each others burdens, and in this way you will fulfill the law of Christ."

While I very much appreciated her card, I fell apart upon receiving it. I knew that Mary must have talked to her after we had talked. I was afraid that Cheryl would feel left out since I hadn't called her to tell her the gory details. The truth is that I knew Cheryl had a lot on her plate at the time, so I had called Mary. I also knew that Mary had taken some psychology and sociology courses while pursuing her nursing degree; I figured she might be able to use some of the things she had gleaned from those courses to help her cope with the awful stuff I was laying on her.

I think that Cheryl's card caught me off guard. I knew it meant that she and Mary had talked to each other. That suggested that they cared about me and were trying to find ways to help me. This idea that my sisters actually cared about me so much was so novel and so foreign it scared me in some way.

I called Carol in tears. When she first heard about Cheryl's card, Carol misinterpreted them as tears of joy to have the support. I tried to explain to her that they were not tears of joy. I didn't know what they were; I didn't know how to handle the support.

I scheduled an extra session with Carol on Monday; I was to meet her Wednesday, but I couldn't wait that long to figure out why I cried every time I tried to read Cheryl's card. I was literally overwhelmed by my sisters' support.

I met with Carol Monday night. I carried both cards with me. I showed her Mary's first. I was able to read it aloud without crying. When I tried to read Cheryl's card to her, I couldn't get beyond the first phrase. This new thing – tangible evidence that my sisters really did love me – was too big for me to comprehend. I didn't know what to do with that love.

I struggled to find a way to express my feelings. I hoped that finding the right words to explain them would help me get a handle on them.

I finally came to recognize it as a fundamental change in what I thought to be the truth about my basic foundation. I named it the tectonic shift; I had experienced an earthquake.

Chapter 9: Tell Them I AM Sent You
February, 2007

*N*ames are powerful. To know someone's name is to have authority over them. I think we all remember a time when our mother called us by our full given name; in my house, that usually meant the one whose name had just been spoken was in a heap of trouble. Some names are not spoken due to a sense of fear so strong that the mere mention of a name conjures terror. For example, most wizards in the Harry Potter series will not speak the name "Lord Voldemort." Either they fear reprisal or they do not want to give Voldemort even more power by mentioning his name.

***

I called Carol in tears. I was overwhelmed and didn't know what to do. This time it wasn't an awful reminder of one of the many horrendous things my grandfather did to me that was so troubling; it was a card from one of my sisters – a card in which she expressed her belief in and love for me and her desire to do whatever she could to help me. My other sister had sent a similar card the day before. Yes, I very much appreciated the sentiment and the support, so I'm sure it's hard to understand how these messages of support could elicit such feelings of unease.

I spent the next week floundering – partially because I felt guilty for not being able to appreciate the support and partially because my world had been shattered – not by my grandfather this time, but by my sisters' support.

The abuse began when I was not yet three and continued for about fourteen years. All that time, my grandfather repeatedly told me how bad I was, how unworthy I was, what a piece of junk I was. I internalized that message and believed that even my own sisters agreed with his assessment. After all, why would their view differ from that of my grandfather? He was the grownup who knew best. Not only did he implant this very strong belief in my basic badness and unworthiness, he also abused me in other awful ways. They were scary, terrible, horrendous and beyond, but I didn't tell anyone because I had been taught that I would be in trouble if anyone found out, that whomever I told wouldn't care, and that none of it mattered anyway because I was such a worthless piece of nothing.

After years of therapy, I began to believe that maybe I wasn't this awful person my grandfather repeatedly told me I was. I reached out to my sisters in new ways, and they responded with the cards. The first card was special; the second sent me reeling, and I didn't know what to do.

About a week after receiving that second card, I found a "name" for what was happening. I called it the "I've just experienced a seismic shift in the tectonic plates that form my own basic understanding of who I am" struggle. In essence, my "California coast" had fallen into the ocean, and the formerly barren parts of the adjacent desert had become very desirable ocean-front properties. It was such a shock to my basis ... my foundation ... the very core of who I knew myself to be was shaken at its innermost basis.

Now, even if the part of the coastline that fell into the ocean was fundamentally flawed from the years of listening to his lies – even if that part needed to be broken down and washed clean by the ocean waters – it still wasn't easy to navigate through what I once knew as desert wasteland after it was transformed from a barren landscape to one robed in lush flora. I simply didn't know the terrain at all, and the earthquake altered the magnetic poles. So, not only was the map wrong following the earthquake, but my basic compass wasn't working correctly either.

Fortunately, I have my guru (Carol) with me on this expedition into the new lands; she's a great guru who can readily adapt to swiftly changing terrain – even with parts of land masses falling into the ocean. She also seems to have a secret "magical" compass that does not rely on the magnetic properties of the poles. I'm also joined in this journey by my husband – a sweet and faithful Sherpa. He doesn't quite grasp the concept that we've just been through a big tremblor, but he's still here steadily walking beside me sharing the load as best as he can.

My sisters are on a completely different planet that is evidently light-years away. They stay in radio contact and provide support from afar. They can't even see the most recent earthquake. In fact, they're still processing data they've received from the last big – and very long and initially hidden – storm. They want to help support me. I want to figure out what I want from them, and I couldn't do that as long as I was struggling with the unknown. Now that I understand what it is – and have named it – I think I'm ready to move on.

***

Oh, the joys of a name. Even though 'the "I've just experienced a seismic shift in the tectonic plates that form my own basic understanding of who I am" struggle' is a long and not very elegant name, it's a name nonetheless. Now that I have a name for it, I can have power over the scary parts and begin to figure them out. It's new terrain – a whole new landscape; I just have to find the right shoes to wear in this newly re-formed land.

***

In Exodus 3, we find the story of Moses and the burning bush. When God called Moses to go to the Israelites in Egypt, Moses replied, "When I tell them 'the God of your fathers sent me to you,' and they ask, 'what is his name?' what do I tell them?" God replies to Moses, "Tell them *I AM* sent you."

Our God is bigger than a name, and our God is here with us – perhaps tangibly in the person of your counselor, perhaps more mystically, perhaps both and more.

May you find names for your troubles, and, once you do, may you begin to figure out how to handle them.

I AM is on your side.

Chapter 10: My Journey Continues
March 2007 and Beyond

Thank you for sharing my journey with me. If you are walking a similar path, I hope that you have a Carol, a Garth, a Cheryl and a Mary, and a Maggie. If you find a Dottie, don't be afraid to move on.

I know there are no magic wands, mystic words, or secret potions that can change the past. The things he did to me will always be a part of who I am. It is what it is, and I am going to be okay in spite of those things.

As bad as they were, I must acknowledge that there are times when I can see something good that has come from the bad. Oh, I don't think God wants or causes bad things to happen to us so we can learn from them. I _do_ believe that God can take even the worst of times and help us find good in them. After all, we find our ultimate salvation through death on a cross.

I wish that it weren't true, but I know there will always be times when an unexpected reminder takes me back to one of the horrible things he did to me. I have learned that it's okay to reach out for help when that happens. It is true that our family and friends want to share our burdens.

I have made so much progress. At the same time, I am not ready to give up my weekly sessions with my mom, Carol. She assures me that I can keep coming as long as I want to be there. I know I'm growing up and the day will come when it is time to step out on my own – to say good-bye to Carol for the last time.

It's not time for that yet. I'll know it when it is.

My journey continues …

www.ingramcontent.com/pod-product-compliance
Lightning Source LLC
Chambersburg PA
CBHW021234280526

45784CB00005B/2100